BLOSSOM

The Art of Sacred Dying

Praise for *Blossom: The Art of Sacred Dying*

"Gerstman tells the powerful, fascinating, and instructive story of how to have a good and sacred death. Befriending Blossom and learning of her terminal diagnosis takes the author on an emotional and informative journey combining the metaphysical and the practical with great compassion and humor. A must-read for all of us as we face our final journey."
—Karen Jones, author of *Death for Beginners*
and *The Summer of Grace*
www.kjwriter.com

"This is an excellent read for anyone seeking insight into the profound journey of life's final stages. Gerstman's book offers a deeply personal and inspiring look at the last nine months of Blossom Flowers Ford Burns' life, sharing her courageous and thoughtful approach to dying. Blossom's story is filled with joy, humor, and the wisdom of embracing mortality with open arms.

"Readers will find valuable lessons on caregiving, community, and the beauty that can emerge even in life's most challenging moments. Gerstman's intimate portrayal of Blossom's life and death provides comfort, guidance, and a fresh perspective on how to face the inevitable with grace. Whether you are a caregiver, healthcare professional, or simply curious about the sacredness of dying, this book is a powerful reminder that death can be the natural, sacred experience it was meant to be with the right education, kindness and support."
—Suzanne B. O'Brien, RN,
Founder of Doulagivers Institute

"In her moving new book, Regina Gerstman shares a deeply personal account of entering, observing, embracing, and ultimately absorbing the multidimensional world of Blossom Flowers Ford Burns, a revered Austin feminist elder who was navigating her last year of life. Transformational themes of spirituality, friendship, social connection, positive awe, loyalty, legacy, and ultimately transcendence are well-represented here. As a friend and colleague of Dr. Gerstman's now for almost fifty years, I've had the continued benefit of directly witnessing the ongoing legacy of Blossom in this author's life. I highly recommend this book to seekers of any age or tradition."
–Susan Raeburn, PhD, clinical psychologist, author (with Eric Maisel),
"Creative Recovery: A Complete Addiction Treatment Program That
Uses Your Natural Creativity" *Shambhala*, 2008

BLOSSOM

The Art of Sacred Dying

REGINA GERSTMAN

Brandylane Publishers, Inc.
Publishing books since 1985

ISBN (Paperback): 978-1-962416-85-6
ISBN (Hardcover): 978-1-962416-86-3
ISBN (eBook): 978-1-962416-87-0
Library of Congress Control Number: 2024927393

Designed by Sami Langston
Project managed by Ashley Barnhill

Printed in the United States of America

Published by
Brandylane Publishers, Inc.
5 S. 1st Street
Richmond, Virginia 23219

Brandylane
Publishers, Inc.
Publishing books since 1985

brandylanepublishers.com

To Leslie and Nan
who saw who I am

To the Buffalo Seminary
which taught me how to write a sentence

To the Raw Carrots Test at the University of Michigan
which identified my potential to be a writer

To the Chesapeake Bay branch of the
National League of American Pen Women
whose members showed me the way

GRACE

I walk in the state of Grace.
I walk in the Eternal Light,
The Great Eternal Light is in me.
I am the Light,
We are one.

I have gone into the Light,
Time stopped as time,
And became Eternal Time.
The Great Silence of Eternity was there.
I know the Absolute Silence.
The Joy and Ecstasies is in the Light,
It is in the Silence, it is the Silence.
And the Great Time stands still.

YOU DO NOT HAVE TO BELIEVE ME,
I invite you to go there yourself.
Go, listen to the sound of Silence,
See the bright, golden, white Light,
Taste the Grand Joy, and the Pure Sweetness.
Then come back and tell me what you know.
I will believe you, but will the others?
Be careful what you say.

You ask me to show you the Way,
You ask me to point to the Path for this Purity,
I say, you only have to die first.

Are you ready to see this Death Angel?
I promise, you will kiss this Presiding Angel.

The Kiss may come when you least expect it,
Prepare your heart now for such Love.
Let us go into this Great Realm together.
I will hold your hand and guide you on the Path,
Do not be afraid, it is safe and miracle filled.

THEN, YOU TRY TO TELL THE OTHERS.

B. Burns

CONTENTS

INTRODUCTION

This is the story of the last nine months of the life of Blossom Flowers Ford Burns. The period is 1998–1999, Austin, Texas. Blossom embodied the mid-century themes of rights movements and women's liberation, which had come to the forefront of society's attention. She was an accomplished artist, yet saw herself as a writer and serious philosopher before identifying with her earlier careers as an art historian, painter, and sculptor. It was her philosophy and approach toward death that inspired the writing of this book. Blossom was ahead of her time in her thoughts about death and her preparation for it. In 2025, many people have since adopted these same practices, but in her era, Blossom had no role model for her choices. She prepared for her death her way. The story of our friendship's development was our first journey. Sharing the last months of her life as they unfolded was our second. Blossom entered my life when I was searching for a connection. We discovered that our lives, like a Venn diagram, had already intersected through friends and activities. Although we shared only a nine-month friendship, we caught each other at a pivotal transition point in each of our lives.

One purpose of *Blossom* is to reflect on a new model of caregiving, at a time when hospice was in a nascent stage in America. On learning of her cancer diagnosis, Blossom organized her friends—or perhaps her friends organized her—to provide the care a single, older woman living alone with serious health issues required. Another purpose is to contrast both the levity and complexity of an older person's life with the joyfulness and laughter, in fact, the sheer fun, that is still possible up until the last moment of life. This small book reflects the role of community for the ill and dying. How many times have we all heard *What do I do? What do*

I say? when we become aware of a relative or friend's fatal illness? Several different styles of interplay are displayed herein. Overall, Blossom's friendship community remained active and engaged, observing with grace.

Although many people interrelated with Blossom throughout her final nine months, this is the story of my experience and connection with her. The others in her community would have a different story to tell and a different connection to this unusual woman. The story of my friendship with Blossom is also the story of a relationship between a mentor and a mentee, which I had not recognized as such at the time. Consumed with my responsibilities, I kept a healthy balance between Blossom and me. Blossom could be needy and demanding. Time spent with her had to be squeezed between perfecting my dissertation, and after that, the sudden emergence of a new teaching position at a university down the road. I carefully selected visits to her that fit my demanding schedule. However, I saw her as an important new friend, a person with whom I had an instant, soul-level connection. She entered my life like a speedboat, pulling me powerfully, and left my life changed in her wake.

This story resonates not only with the personal but also the professional. Students taking human development and Death and Dying courses could benefit from and enjoy this story, which can serve to supplement didactic information and training about the end of life. Healthcare professionals and workers within the medical community could learn from this book as well. The many Carl G. Jung societies and associations sprinkled throughout the United States could also expand on Blossom's thinking in their seminars. People of all ages who are caring for or are terminally ill could also benefit from this unusual story, which weaves the metaphysical into the practical realities of one's last months and days as seen through the eyes of a friendship.

As I gather my memories and recollect, I hope to not only describe our friendship but also point out what is important and meaningful about our time together. I recall my experience with Blossom as a privileged time in my life. I was privileged to know this woman, however briefly, at the apex of her mental abilities, who bathed in the brilliance of her total life experience. Entering Blossom's *queendom* was an opportunity for learning, deep thinking, mystical revelation, and codifying metaphysical theory. Through the experience she shared with me over the last months of her life, Blossom taught me the difference between the *good* death and the *sacred* death, and she gave me the push to take a leap and really live life. I was transformed.

THE NARRATIVE OCTAVE

CHAPTER 1

THE GREEK RESTAURANT PARTY

I was running a little late for my shift at the Jung Society of Austin's monthly meeting. This month, in late July, we were celebrating Carl Jung's birthday at the Sixth Street Greek Restaurant. I had offered to help Ruby Scott, the executive director, at the door—take tickets, mark off attendees, and sell tickets. We had all been promised delicious Greek specialties, a short meeting, and a dance band. I ran to my car in the 101-degree wet heat and drove downtown as quickly as I could.

The restaurant was extremely dark when I entered. I had to duck under some hanging curtains to get from the door inside to the room. To my left was a long table, and Ruby abruptly pulled me to a spot beside her, had me sit, and left me to monitor admissions while she immediately took a break. After a rush of latecomers, things at the door began to settle down, and I finally had a chance to look around. The room was crowded. The stage, with amplifiers and a microphone in front, was located at the center back, as chairs and tables adorned with small candles in glass containers wrapped the boundary of the space.

Feeling a sense of disorientation, I tried to locate a friend to talk with, searching for my place in this group. Looking up, I saw the older female Jungian therapists sitting and chatting at a table. These women did not return a hello when I smiled at them. Feeling rebuffed, I wondered if this group was a good fit for me, and I continued to search for a like-minded soul. Ruby returned and introduced me to her husband. We chatted for a few moments, and I felt a bit more comfortable. Suddenly, as in a fairy tale, there was a stir at the door.

A short woman with a fantastic mass of white hair poking out from beneath a black felt cowboy hat walked slowly toward the entrance. She used a cane to steady herself. She was surrounded by a group of at least five younger women in their forties. She must have been twenty-five or thirty years older. Once she was clearly inside the doorway, I was struck by her unusual appearance. Dressed completely in black long sleeves and pants, the only color on her was a bright red necklace of large Indian mala beads hanging long from her neck and her thick red lipstick. She came swooshing in, the girls chattering around her as if protecting her. One woman checked off their names, paid, and the group proceeded to an empty table and sat all around it.

I turned to Ruby, "Who is that?" It was as much a question as an exclamation.

"Oh, that's Blossom," she stated in a rather dismissive manner.

"Blossom?"

"Yes, she is an old member who has recently rejoined the Jung, returning from Virginia."

"And who are all these younger women with her?"

"Her friends, her followers, her *students*," she answered somewhat sarcastically.

I watched the group for a little while and then was recruited to help pour the punch. I ate delicious grape leaves and baklava and danced with the group in the crowded central area of the room. As people began to leave and the room thinned out, I pulled a chair to the outer row of Blossom's table to discover what was encouraging the attentiveness from her coterie. Then I too looked at Blossom's face. I saw a bright, shiny apple complexion, youthful and smooth, her brown eyes alive with dominance and intelligence. She seemed exuberant and in her element, holding court with her subjects. Blossom immediately asked me who I was and then introduced me to her group of friends.

I struggled to understand the conversation but slowly realized Blossom was talking about time, one of her favorite subjects. I believe she was trying to make the point that the concept of time is quite meaningless, that everything in our awareness is occurring in the present. I wondered if the other women could make sense of her comments. Shortly after I had joined the group, it began to break up. Before Blossom rose and was escorted out by one or two of her friends, she asked for my phone number and said I was to come for tea Sunday afternoon. I expressed tentativeness to accept because my time was already committed to preparing for my final oral defense. Being awarded my doctorate in educational psychology depended on my performance in a few weeks. Completely ignoring my hesitancy, Blossom said she would call me ahead of time to give directions. Tomorrow was Sunday, and all I could think about was meeting my deadlines.

"Where do you live?" she asked.

"On Fielding Road," I answered.

"That is right around the corner from me! I will see you at two" she declared.

So, it was decided. I had moved forward two steps; Blossom had surged ten.

CHAPTER 2

TEA AND HOMEWORK: A SCHOLARLY INITIATION

I had scheduled a visit to Blossom between one and two in the afternoon. When I called around ten in the morning, I was emphatic that I could visit for only an hour. There was too much on my plate! I finished my maintenance tasks and phone calls to my family. I prepared the astrology chart of a woman who had just died by suicide, to try to understand what had happened. And I promised myself I would take a walk after my visit with Blossom. Despite the pressures, I was looking forward to visiting with this eccentric woman.

It turned out that I was exactly one mile from Blossom's home on Benstone Drive. Benstone was an easement, and therefore quite narrow, with a brushy cliff across the road from most of the six houses there, slanting down to Shoal Creek. Many people walked and jogged on the footpath next to the creek. I parked in the street and looked up to Blossom's small studio house, which was built into the hill. This studio was just beneath a larger, two-story Frank Lloyd Wright house replica built on Blossom's property farther up the hill.

As you approached the studio, there was a narrow winding path of stone steps with a thin railing to grasp. *Studio* is a misnomer, for this smaller home had twelve rooms, though all of them quite small, and a hallway which zigzagged between the sections of the house. The entryway required me to pass through a wooden lattice-framed garden at the side of the studio with a large Japanese fishpond also built into the hill, pump, and hose lying on the piled stones. The first door to the studio opened into a large mudroom, with shelves of trains, dog figurines, and other pieces of eclectic, cheap *objets d'art,* all spray painted in gold, occupying the window crannies or displayed on a ceiling balcony shelf. Off to the side of this room was another room enclosed in ceiling-to-floor windows. This was Blossom's sculpting studio where she had once created her artwork. Peeking in, I could see huge busts of *Mother Clasping Child to Belly, Mexican Child*, and others lined in a row peeking out from a partly shrouded table.

At the next door, six feet across the mudroom, I rang the bell. Blossom beamed an enormous smile and brought me into the small hallway. She referred to this area as the library. It was filled with narrow shelves built into the walls and a few skinny stand-alone bookcases stuffed with her philosophy and art books. She invited me into the living room, located at the side of the house looking out toward the street, which had a more organized array of larger shelves, and books, books, books. The walking distance between the two small armchairs on the right side of the living room and the couch on the left, with a low coffee table between, could have passed for a hoarder's path. Passing another person in this home would involve twisting the upper body and squeezing one's feet as far to the opposite side as possible. Blossom told me to sit while she proceeded to prepare the tea.

A carpeted step at the end of the living room led to another room filled with books, hassocks, a square table, a chair, and then to the kitchen. The kitchen seemed to hang in the trees, with green leaves on branches floating toward and resting on the kitchen windows. From the kitchen window I could look out over the street, along the treetops, and see the creek and its pathway down below. It was beautiful! The tea kettle was boiling, and Blossom had set a tray with a teapot and two cups and saucers ready to serve. She filled the teapot with the boiling water and picked up her tray to return to the living room. I scurried back to my seat. As she instructed, we waited seven minutes before pouring the tea. "But you Americans don't know how to make real tea, as they do in India." Her first admonishment. Well, I was willing to observe and learn.

"Oh, I forgot the cookies." Blossom returned to the kitchen and fetched a prepared plate with four or five almond lemon cookies on it. She sat down. For the next hour and then some, Blossom spoke about her life, her health, and her boyfriend during adolescence, who was now the love of her life! Although she politely asked about my dissertation topic, she really wanted to share her story. So, I listened and learned. Blossom said she had spent the past four years living in Virginia because her childhood boyfriend, her *true husband*, was there, whom she called the Colonel.

"Your true husband?"

"Yes, I am more of a woman and he is more of a man when we are together."

Later I learned that the Colonel, Paul, had met Blossom in high school after her family had moved from Oklahoma to Fort Worth. He was drawn to her quizzical face and active mind. He towered over her yet felt she was striking despite her minute stature. Blossom reminded him of his mother, who was a professor of geology at the University of Texas, a trailblazer despite the gender bias of the time. They each had a first meeting story. By Paul's account, after he had first approached Blossom, he knew he could read her, and she knew she could trust him. By Blossom's account, related in a prose poem called "Soul Mates," after a short interchange she ended up walking away with him into "a strange and tragic romance." Blossom talked about Paul as being the top man in their high school class, commanding respect from his classmates because he embodied fairness, intelligence, athleticism, and kindness. They were together for all the events and outings throughout the rest of their high school years. Paul studied analytic geometry at UT Austin after his first year at Virginia Military Institute so that he could "study" Blossom who was attending college there. Although they were still pledged to each other through the separations during their remaining college years, they ended up marrying other partners.

"And what brings you back home to Austin, Blossom?"

"I needed to take care of my house and my health." She mentioned some serious repairs the foundation needed and that the bamboo forest along one whole side of both houses needed to be thinned and cut back. I had a feeling there might be more to the story.

All around the studio, there were sculptures and framed artwork. I asked about her paintings and huge clay busts, but she had no interest in describing that part of her work. She explained that her main medium was writing. She had been a writer her entire life, composing poetry during childhood and adolescence and over the past four years in Virginia. Painting was important in her college years when she studied art history. She earned a master's degree in art history and taught this field "down the road." By *down the road,* she meant she traveled twenty-seven miles to teach at Southwest Texas State University in San Marcos, another giant school of 38,000 students like the University of Texas at Austin. I admired her courage to work in the arts, having been dissuaded in my own late childhood from furthering my interest in piano performance.

In this first encounter, Blossom did not speak in detail about her health. She shared she had heart disease and only briefly mentioned that part of her decision to return home was because her diabetes had gotten out of control. She wanted to see her longtime doctors. Blossom poured the tea into the cups and handed me a saucer.

"Take a cookie, take a cookie." I was a good guest and enjoyed her snack.

I looked around at my surroundings. "Blossom, why are there iron bars across all the windows in the house?"

Blossom explained that after her years teaching art and art history, she returned to graduate school at the University of Texas for a master's degree in classical Hindu and Buddhist studies in the philosophy department. During this time, she became a devotee of Dr. Gupta V. Desani, an Indian scholar who was teaching there. She referred to him as the Professor. I began to see that the main people in Blossom's life would be referred to by their roles or titles, like players in the board game Clue, with their professions substituting for their names. Blossom was letting me know she does things her way. She had invited the Professor to live in the studio while she lived upstairs in her big house. He was extremely successful, but his popularity caused jealousy and he developed some enemies. If there had been an incident, Blossom did not share it. In any case, the two of them decided to make the studio more secure for him. It seemed so strange to me that in a small crowded house full of unusual sculptures and books, thick iron bars crossed all its windows, much like at a zoo! I mentioned to Blossom that I knew a woman of Indian descent, Suri, who was a fellow student and friend. We met at the university four years ago when we began our studies in the educational psychology program. Blossom eagerly requested I bring Suri the next time I visited.

I had shared over the phone with Blossom that I had constructed an astrology chart that morning of a well-known woman in Austin who had committed suicide at the beginning of the week. I was still disturbed by this sad event. Blossom asked me how I came to be knowledgeable about astrology. I recounted the history in brief: self-study, tedious creation of charts by hand, attendance at a ten-day intensive training to become professionalized by a respected mother-daughter duo of psychologist-astrologers, and the purchase of software once the field was computerized. I had also spent the last five years working the psychic fairs and seeing private clients. I loved that she was not judgmental or in any way disdaining this field of study or my expertise. She knew the value and the difficulty of the field. In her mind, it was no discredit to me to be a clinician, an educator, a researcher, and an astrologer. She saw these skills as an asset. In Blossom's mind, I was a scholar.

When I rose to leave, I peeked down the narrow hallway to the back section of the house, "the apartment." All I could see was a center door, a bathroom, and a room off to each side of it.

"Wait, before you go, I have something for you." Blossom turned to reach behind the couch and began leafing through folders of articles and papers stacked on top of books. She finally found what she was looking for and asked me to read an article so that we could discuss it the next time I saw her.

"What is it about?" I asked because its meaning was not apparent from the title.

"Lord Shiva."

Being a neophyte, I figured I would read the article, per her request. As I turned to leave, she said I should call one of her Jungian friends for details or questions about the homework.

What an unusual new friend! As I jumped into my car, I realized I was now becoming one of Blossom's students, as I had heard about the night before. I knew no one at all like her and thoroughly enjoyed my first visit to her studio. The mentor-mentee relationship was beginning, and I vowed to make the time to read this forty-page, single-spaced behemoth, committed to continuing this adventure with my new friend.

CHAPTER 3

The Prayer Room Revealed

Blossom began to call me a few times a week, and we would talk for ten or fifteen minutes. She always opened up with some news about the Colonel. If he was coming, if he had just left after an extended visit, how happy he made her. In one of our chats, Blossom was keen to remind me that she wanted to meet my friend Suri and asked how that plan was coming along. It took me about a month to coordinate our schedules so that I could finally bring Suri to meet Blossom. Since the loss of the Professor, it seemed Blossom wanted to continue her connection to Indian culture with the hope of fostering a friendship with Suri.

Suri drove to my apartment one Sunday afternoon in August, looking forward to meeting someone who knew something about her homeland. She did not seem very happy today. When I inquired, I got an earful of disgust about her husband, soon to be her ex-husband. She believed that as a professor at the university, he should be held to a higher standard! I agreed with her and hoped she would begin to feel calmer. I expressed how sorry I was she was experiencing this chaotic time in her life. She really was most upset about the example her husband was providing to their son, who was ten years old. Suri and I were both in transition: she in her marriage, and I in my education and career.

We went downstairs to my small Camry and drove over to Blossom's. Blossom welcomed us, had us sit, and brought out the tea. She turned to Suri and said, "I am serving *real* tea," and Suri responded with a knowing nod. For the second time, Blossom cackled about Americans who pretend to know how to prepare tea. They enjoyed a moment of superiority over me. Then Blossom shifted slightly to look directly at her newest contact and grew more serious. She began to ask questions: where Suri was born, what her parents did, where she received her education, and how long she had been in America. Although Suri quickly answered *Delhi, civil servant, housekeeper,* and the names of her American universities, her first significant words to Blossom were a pronouncement that she would never marry again. What followed was a harangue against Hindu astrologers! I was stunned by the ferocity of Suri's disdain. Apparently, she had consulted one before each of her two unhappy marriages and bristled with regret for listening to the prognosticators each time. Blossom piped up, "Well, Regina knows how to make astrology charts!" I explained that Western astrology was quite different from Hindu astrology and that I was aware of some of the basics of the more ancient tradition. Suri continued her attacks against men, against astrology, and a tad against me! I was thinking of defending myself when Blossom jumped in and addressed Suri, "I can read you right now. I do not need a chart. Your soul is crying!"

Reaching out and empathizing seemed to soften Suri, who then admitted she felt lost. But she immediately followed with how grateful she was that her son provided a purpose, an anchor around which to organize her tasks. She asked Blossom for advice on how to spend time with her son, of whom she was the custodial parent. Blossom quickly suggested standard good parenting activities: going to the library, reading together, and doing the things he enjoyed. I believed Blossom could communicate with anyone using her laser intelligence and emotional insight, as she had just displayed in her deft handling of a suffering soul. Blossom knew nothing about Suri nor the offense of her husband, but her kindness and ability to transcend the actual conversation with a more metaphysical analysis transformed Suri's wall of defensiveness and anger into a willingness to open up about her inner world. Like a seasoned psychotherapist, Blossom understood to wrap up the description of Suri's trauma with an overriding empathic redirect. They formed a connection, and I was captivated.

Blossom continued to talk about her memories of life with

the Professor at the studio. He and Blossom had decided to turn a section of the living room into a prayer room. It was then that I realized what lay behind the wall, located down a little alley between the couch and the fireplace, turning into an enclosed space directly behind the couch. She explained that he had many followers and often held an open house during the week, somewhat akin to holding office hours but in this studio. She was his student at first before becoming his landlady, studying ancient Hindu and Buddhist philosophy. She was quick to add that her work with the Professor was not the philosophy Americans think of and usually study in college as Indian philosophy, that this was *real* classical Hindu and Buddhist philosophy. I asked for examples of the differences between the two courses of study. Blossom offered no explanation. In the pause that followed, I wondered if I was expected to understand her meaning and to learn from her wisdom through osmosis! I began to see that Blossom was living her idea about time, staying focused on the immediate present, of its experience rather than any lengthy discourse or small talk.

"Would you show us the prayer room, Blossom?" I asked.

Blossom rose to get the key, as the small room's door was kept locked. Well, finding the key became her next task! Down the narrow alley was a tiny desk against the wall facing the kitchen, with a chair tucked in and mounds of papers and paperclips strewn about. This was the office. The shelves above the desk had dolls from foreign countries, special items from Blossom's life, and pictures of her sons and the Professor. The key was hidden in a little aluminum pie dish with other clips and coins.

"I've got it!"

We were in line behind Blossom eager to peek in. She opened the door, and bright sunlight streamed in from a high window on the outer side of the room. It warmed my face as I glanced excitedly from ceiling to floor. All four walls had large cotton Indian bedspreads tacked up above mounds of pillows lying on long narrow benches against each wall. Covering the floor were many brightly colored pillows, some inset with little pieces of diamond-shaped glass shining from the fabric. Blossom immediately told us we could not enter; only one person was allowed in at a time, and the room was as she had left it. She turned to close and lock the door. We filed backward out of the office area and sat down again in the living room. I felt an inner thrill of having viewed her sacred prayer space. "Blossom, when was the last time you were in the prayer room?" Blossom turned to me and answered that she tried to go in daily for meditation, although recently she had been very busy with doctors' appointments.

After a little more chit-chat, Suri needed to start for home, as her son would be dropped off soon. I stood and we bid our goodbyes. Blossom was very happy that we had come to visit and said she would be talking to me soon. I noticed she did not give Suri the initiation homework, perhaps assuming an Indian woman already knew about Lord Shiva. I promised her I would give her Suri's phone number in our next call. During this visit, Blossom showed more of her character and personal life than at our first. As an elder seeking friends, Blossom also revealed her most private space for communicating with the One. Blossom's mystique was enveloping me. I felt we had entered a new level of intimacy, and I was eager to open more of myself to her.

CHAPTER 4

THE CAREGIVERS

By the end of September, my biweekly visits to my new friend embodied a different focus and meaning. Blossom had recently learned from her doctor that she had pancreatic cancer. The Colonel was visiting at the time, and Blossom had spread the word among her Jungian friends. One of her friends organized a schedule for others to care for Blossom during the evenings, spend the nights, and help her in the mornings. It was incredible how quickly a monthly calendar was set up, and each month people filled in their time commitments. The calendars were tacked on the first wall one saw in the library on entering the studio. Behind that wall, Blossom had her large bedroom with a bathroom in the back right corner. Next to her room, the caregivers could sleep in the small back apartment room and use the tiny bathroom at the end of the hall. I was now in the middle of a rapidly developed makeshift caregiving arrangement, and the studio had acquired a more serious tone. In my mind, I called these women, and the few men, *death transition workers.* Their network was seamless and filled with a confident knowledge of the soul work they were doing.

When I first learned of Blossom's new health status, I immediately proclaimed I could not stay overnight, because I had accepted my first teaching job at the Southwest Texas State University psychology department, a half-hour down the road from Austin. Yes, I had been awarded my doctorate after my final oral defense, and the very next day I was offered this choice position. Climb one mountain, back to the bottom in an instant. I had courses to prepare, and it was already late August! I did, however, continue my visits, stopping by about twice a week. One week I noticed a small sign tacked above the headboard of Blossom's bed, which read,

PLEASE DO NOT CALL EMS.
I DO NOT WISH TO BE RESUSCITATED.

This sign reflected Blossom's conscious choice to die in her own house under the care of her friends, rather than among strangers and machines. I thought of a friend, Ann, who could possibly help. Ann was already a volunteer with hospice who worked with the seriously ill and those close to death. She was currently living in an older man's home to care for him as he became more infirm. She was always a flexible person willing to do something new, so when I asked her to meet Blossom, she was immediate in her response.

Although I had coordinated their get-together, I was not present. I thought they had enough in common to readily connect and help each other. Both women were raised in Texas, had disapproving parents, and suffered through very unhappy childhoods, yet emerged strong, intellectual, opinionated adults. Their differences included their stage of life, overall health, and home life: Blossom was divorced and had two sons, with a surviving son who was struggling, and Ann was married and had one daughter who was flourishing. Blossom needed help as an older woman with serious health problems, and Ann, in her young forties, had spent several years attending to older people in need of special care. I thought the two women would be a perfect match!

Ann visited Blossom on a midweek evening by herself after her usual walk around Town Lake. Blossom recounted some of her life to Ann, giving the impression that her parents had not cared for her and that she therefore grew up a loner who had escaped into her writing, poetry, and artwork. Ann responded that her father, very much alive and a presiding district judge in rural Texas, rejected his daughter's educational aspirations, most of her interests, and any of her opinions resembling feminist ideology.

Her mother had an *unnatural* relationship with the meekest of her three sons as well as a boyfriend who often stayed with her at the house. Ann emerged from this family as a strong, ardent, beautiful woman with conventional opinions of how things should and should not be in the world. It seemed obvious to me that these two very Southern ladies, both surviving Faulkneresque childhoods, could relate to each other.

According to Blossom, there was yelling, standing up, and attempts to leave. The pitta was flying, I was told. I hadn't understood the Ayurvedic reference but soon learned that *pitta* refers to one's inner fire. In the end, they somehow reconciled, and Ann helped Blossom and read to her. She also organized Blossom's voluminous pills. The next time I visited the studio, I saw Ann's name on the monthly schedule of caregivers, visiting four hours per week through Hospice House. Ann also drove Blossom to chemotherapy treatments, and they would stop at Luby's, her favorite cafeteria, for a snack. I felt I had contributed in a small way to Blossom's safe and continuous care community by introducing a person who was already on my path and was now on Blossom's.

On another of my visits, Blossom talked about the new health regime given to her by Caitlyn, a local chiropractor, who was advising homeopathic treatments not only for Blossom's pancreatic cancer but also for her diabetes and heart disease. When I asked Blossom how she had come to know Caitlyn, she responded that for many years, before her time in Virginia, she had belonged to the Austin chapter of IANDS. I asked her what this was, and Blossom explained,

"The International Association of Near-Death Studies."

"Oh my goodness, Blossom. Are you talking about Caitlyn O'Manly and Ned Sarumby?"

"Absolutely! Do you know them?"

"Caitlyn was one of the first people I met in Austin right after I moved here in the summer of 1993. I met her at an integrative health exposition. We have been friends for five years. I have heard all about both of their near-death experiences, in great detail, as they asked me to make charts and do readings about their experiences. Blossom, this is amazing how our worlds in Austin have overlapped!"

I pondered my own statement: I had shared my life path with Blossom and now she was introducing me to healers on her path, causing intersections previously unknown but also known, and creating new crossroads as members of the same thriving community. As my life intersected with Blossom's, the community developing around her passing was extending to those flourishing in the community of the living.

Caitlyn and Ned usually came together to sit with Blossom and stay over one of the weekend nights. The three together talked about death and philosophy, levels of consciousness, the meaning of the soul, and the possibility of reincarnation—all of Blossom's favorite topics. It was only a matter of time before I ran into them at the studio. It seemed Blossom was attracting the most interesting people in the community. By interesting, I mean people who were drawn to the metaphysical, who knew there was something more than day-in, day-out waking awareness: people who would reflect to Blossom the sparkle she always seemed to have in her eyes. On one weekend, Caitlyn and Ned took Blossom to a seminar at the Westlake Bank Community Group Room. The local hospice had a committee called Compassion in Action, and they had hired a woman from Los Angeles to come to Austin to host this group meeting and train people in end-of-life care. The homework was to read any of Dannion Brinkley's books, written to help people change their consciousness about dying. Caitlyn, Ned, and Blossom were on a mission to learn the latest about dying with dignity, especially since all of them had undergone near-death experiences that left them feeling out of control.

I visited Blossom after she had attended the seminar. She was alone, waiting for her evening caregiver. She stated she was completely exhausted and would not be capable of sharing about the meeting at this time. This had happened once before when I came back to discuss the journal article on Lord Shiva. Blossom waved a hand, paying the topic no mind, and continued with the moment-to-moment agenda of her survival. The message was clear:

being together and sharing the moments with knowing looks and little laughs were more important than esoteric spinning. Our friendship was building trust. Trust and patience. The preciousness of being present.

Another devoted caregiver was her young friend Dina. When I crossed paths with her at Blossom's one late afternoon, she said she remembered meeting me at the Greek restaurant. As I sat there, I realized Dina looked exactly like Blossom had in a portrait of her as an adolescent girl, which hung in the eating area! Dina provided a jolt of youthful energy and fun to Blossom and was invaluable in keeping her spirit alive. They often watched movies together late into the night while eating forbidden treats—forbidden to a diabetic, that is.

There were also the analysts from the Jung who fed Blossom's intellectual and spiritual nature. The eldest was Geralyn, a tall, thin, greying woman who sported glasses and long straight skirts—Blossom held her in great respect and included her in many of her major decisions. Geralyn was a diplomate in analytic psychology. She had completed her training at the Jung Institute in Zurich and had a large clientele in Austin. Her close friend Hannah was not a trained analyst but was included in the group of five or six women from the Jung who considered themselves the most serious practitioners of Jungian theory in their therapy practices. Hannah was vivacious, opinionated like Blossom, and a good team player. Both women were on the schedule of overnight caregivers.

There were many others, too. Ned had recruited volunteers from the IANDS chapter of which he was president, most of whom lived in the Hill Country, southwest of Austin, or more rurally, out toward San Marcos. As a group, they possessed an inner sensitivity and beauty that radiated to all the people in their lives. Being a companion to Blossom during her illness became a community activity in which each member felt responsible for her compassionate care's success. I do not recall an evening in which Blossom was absent a caregiver. That is how tightly this community web was woven.

CHAPTER 5

A Tale of Two Sons

What I observed so far: Blossom had two sons. Kyle was the first born followed by his younger brother, Henry. Kyle's parents considered him the proverbial *golden child*. Earlier, I had noticed an altar in the front room resting on a waist-high bookcase against the windows facing the creek. It consisted of an eighteen-inch Koa wood plate, and from left to right: a photograph of Kyle in his young twenties, some special stones, a photograph of the Professor, and finally, a framed picture of one of Blossom's poems, "In Praise of a Living Guru." It was clear that special care had been taken in the selection and arrangement of these objects on the platform set on the left side of the bookcase. So, if one were eating at the larger square table and looked forward, one would first see this altar and then, beyond, the grand expanse of treetops outside with the Shoal Creek ravine below.

"Well, Kyle looks healthy, happy, and handsome in that picture, Blossom!"

"That was taken by a friend just before Kyle fell out of an open bed of a pickup truck in Mexico."

"In Mexico—was he okay?"

"No, he cracked his skull and died!"

"Oh my God, Blossom!"

"He was with two of his longtime high school friends. I do not know what they were doing."

I noticed her minimizing the import of her memory and tried to ignore the question stuck in my mind.

"Blossom, was Kyle on a drug run with his friends?" There was no reason for me to assume this—my intuition was following the information given. I think Blossom mumbled around for an answer. I looked away. There was a brief silent interlude, both of us digesting the information—I, for the first time, and Blossom, a tad reluctant and saddened to revisit these events. I now understood the importance of the altar, the crystals, and the picture of the Professor, whom Blossom had elevated to the status of *guru* in her poem. Apparently, Kyle had been successful at everything he touched—the apple of his mother's eye. However, a few misguided decisions on a weekend journey ended it all in an instant. I did not continue probing this topic.

"And where is Henry?" I asked.

"Yes, Henry is hard to pinpoint at any one location. Apparently, he travels up and down the State of California, going from one construction job to the next. Last I heard he was in northern California." I thought, wow, although he was raised in a privileged home, Blossom's surviving son lives the lifestyle of a seasonal worker, a nomad who is uncertain of his next paycheck!

"So how do you keep in touch? Have you ever heard from him?"

"Unfortunately, right now, I hear from Henry infrequently. We have a long history of this kind of communication. He usually calls every month or so, or when he needs something, and then I know he remembers who his mother is." Blossom continued, "He was in college when his brother fell and died." She intimated that the event ended Henry's college career.

"Do you have his phone number, and when was the last time you heard from him? Does he know you have cancer?" I thought it was important for Blossom to let him know about her medical condition. I knew, however, that this woman would decide what she was or was not going to do, so I let the subject drop. It seemed to me that Blossom was harboring a great sadness in her heart about her two sons. I believed her story about Kyle, but I felt there must be more to Henry's life. In our brief exchange about this son, it seemed to me that Blossom felt weary of her whole relationship with him, as she felt cast by him into an obligatory role of never-ending dependency. She explained that another part of her weariness was her prior attempts to encourage a commitment to an interest and to stick with it. There was no getting around it: her no-nonsense attitude about both sons was the result of these tragedies. I was stunned by these personal losses. The golden child, dead in an instant while perhaps doing something not so golden, is no longer there for Blossom to feel proud of and to validate her mothering. And the nomad, with his intransigent connection, was in touch only when he needed something from his mother. The story of Blossom's sons had put a crack in her soul. The psychotherapist in me began to conclude that Blossom had developed a community of close friendships with women in their forties to fill the space her sons no longer did. She needed to share her love, sweetness, and knowledge with young adults, fostering connections and exchanges of respect, appreciation, and admiration. For some, she provided a motherly wisdom.

This visit was not a long one, but it showed me a deeper part of Blossom, more of her life story, and some critical and tragic events. My bond with Blossom strengthened in her sharing about Kyle and Henry, learning intimate details of her life. I wondered if it was common practice for her to minimize her feelings about her losses or if this was a welcomed close moment with someone she could trust. Was Kyle's death the beginning of her slow pivot from art history to philosophy? Had life turned Blossom into a philosopher? Was this why she had the entire collection, all thirty-seven volumes, of Swedenborg's writings on her shelves?

CHAPTER 6

BLOSSOM'S BOOKS

Emanuel Swedenborg (1688–1772)—whom I knew nothing about nor had ever heard of—was an eighteenth-century Swedish philosopher considered by many to be a mystic. Listed among his occupations are mining engineer, anatomist, astronomer, inventor, and author. Located in the skinny studio office, above her desk, a leather-bound collection of Swedenborg's works was for Blossom a source of depth and pride. I tried to pull one of the volumes every few visits and glance through it. Each volume had a simple title, such as *Home, Family, Community, Love.* The volume entitled *Life Between Death and Rebirth* (recommended at the annual IANDS conference in Philadelphia) recounted the story of traveling Swedenborgian minister John Chapman who used the symbol of apple seeds to spread Swedenborg's ideas of rebirth, originating the American myth of none other than Johnny Appleseed. This work in particular reflected the kinship Blossom felt with Swedenborg, validating her own near-death experience as well as her philosophy that death was a part of life.

Like the layers of different styles of architecture in the house and studio, Blossom's shelves divulged the layers of her knowledge. I had noticed the prominence of books in the house when I first set foot inside, and Blossom illustrated the importance of her collection of books in almost every visit, and every discussion. Through learning, studying, and evaluating, she had developed into a scholar of Eastern philosophy, and the evidence was all around. I once asked and Blossom replied, "I have read every book in this house!" I raised my eyebrows but did not reply, as the honesty of scholarship resonated with me, and she knew it. Our friendship could develop further because we both respected knowledge and integrated what we had learned from our lives through experiences and academics. What was different about Blossom, however, was that she was able to connect a great amount of the world's knowledge, bits and pieces from many philosophies, and integrate it all into her own religious cosmology.

Among all of Blossom's books, Swedenborg's works had become her obsession. I wondered if Blossom would become such a legend herself. And what exactly is a mystic? I heard her speak about Swedenborg only to Caitlyn, Ned, and me. Her first connection to Swedenborg I recognized was their ability to master several fields. The second, they were both prodigies of the metaphysical. Swedenborg, as he aged, became interested in everything invisible to the eye, primarily from a religious, and then later, a spiritual point of view. His evolution was right up Blossom's alley. She had dedicated her late adulthood and midlife to the study of Eastern philosophies, their beginnings, and their original meanings, and she spent her midlife teaching classical Hinduism and Buddhism as she understood them. She was primed to ponder the important questions of the human condition. Frequent topics included: *How Could I Be Afraid of Dying* and *Soul Secrets: The Nature of Time.*

Another of Blossom's passions was the work of mythologist Joseph Campbell and his archivist, Jonathan Young. Campbell contributed to the metaphysical, literary, and Jungian communities through his study and knowledge of every mythology created in our world's written history. He extracted the themes and synthesized the message: *There is only one story.* Blossom had read and kept many of Campbell's books in the house, and during one of our visits, I mentioned to her that I had gone to the Jung for a weekend workshop with Young. In our discussion about this workshop, I repeated Campbell's dictum, and we locked eyes and shared a knowing nod of agreement. Young had entitled his program The Symbolic Quest, in which he interweaved the purpose of living in a community with the heroic journey of finding oneself, speaking to the role our chosen communities play along our path. As I shared my excitement and attraction to Dr. Young's breadth of knowledge and gentleness with Blossom, she looked directly into my eyes and stated: "No one is good enough for Dr. Young!" As usual, the master of awareness had spoken and abruptly concluded our discussion.

Young's topic was pure Blossom, as she was always searching, always looking deeper and behind surface meanings, examining symbols, and synthesizing the true meaning. For example, she was drawn to the story of the mother and daughter Demeter and Persephone, and she learned how to understand and reinterpret their fate as Greek mythology recounted it. She trusted her own interpretation of these archetypal stories, and I learned as we talked that Blossom identified with Persephone, the daughter who was raped by the god of the underworld, Hades, and with the full knowledge of her father, Zeus (ruler of the world). She is forced to live in one world, hell, for part of the year, and in the other, above ground, for the rest of the year. She is in both the ordinary world and somewhere beyond. Persephone has been associated with the cycle of life and death, meaning there is life in death and death in life. Friends of Blossom's were fully aware that she too could straddle worlds, waking reality, and metaphysical reality. And, as she coped with her illness, she had no barrier between being alive and the path to death. Delving deeper, the near-death studies community in Austin saw this myth as a perfect telling of the notion of death and rebirth.

Blossom's books were a mirror of who she was. She well understood what Campbell proclaimed: there is only one story—in thousands of stories in their protected and tattered covers. Campbell meant that all myths are some form of describing the arc from birth to death. This journey involves first learning and growing, then venturing out into the world to discover one's gifts, and last, returning home to teach them. Blossom had given a lifetime of her gifts in many forms, especially those of teaching, artistic creation, and writing. At this juncture, it seemed to me she was still searching for a final gift to her community and her friends.

CHAPTER 7

CHRISTMAS AT BLOSSOM'S

The night before Christmas, Blossom called me and asked, "What are you doing tomorrow?" I told her I really had no big plans, and that I was meeting Suri for a joint potluck dinner at my apartment around four in the afternoon. Blossom replied that she was having an open house and wanted me to come: "Bring Suri and your food!" So, I called Suri, who had also received the same invitation. Therefore, once again, we changed course to celebrate with this somewhat disruptive woman.

We entered the mudroom to the studio side door, finding the narrow hallway already packed full of people. They were standing, mulling, viewing the vast collection of art and philosophy books stacked in bookcases throughout the hallway. They were drinking cider and roaming between the kitchen and Blossom's bedroom, where she was holding court in her sleigh bed while either lying in repose, meditating, or sitting upright and entertaining a few of her guests. I placed my bean salad on the kitchen table, greeted a few people, and made my way to Blossom's bedside. I only knew two or three people there as friends—Caitlyn and Ned among them. I recognized several others from meetings of the Jung Society of Austin or as Blossom's friends who stayed overnight with her when they could. When I entered Blossom's bedroom, I saw a young Indian man named Gopa standing by the bed and talking with her. "I'm not afraid of dying," Blossom stated matter-of-factly to Gopa, "It is the next phase of life and I am fully prepared."

In fact, in a recent newspaper interview, Blossom had shared her vast knowledge and beliefs about early Indian Hindu and Buddhist philosophies with the whole town. In the article and this very evening, she was inviting people to her funeral, whenever that might be, and asking them to organize a celebration of her life. She was using her illness and her inevitable fate to educate everyone. She grew more emphatic throwing her arms in the air when I entered the now-crowded bedroom. It felt so crowded because of the huge family heirloom sleigh bed on which she rested in the very center of the bedroom, with ceiling-to-floor burnt-orange velour curtains hanging behind her and a huge cathode ray TV and armchair set in a row at one side of the bed.

She wanted me to meet Gopa. "He is a true Brahmin from India," she told me, pointing with the top of her white-bouffant head toward Gopa. "Your friend Suri has worked her way up from the civil servant class and married above her station. Gopa, he's the real thing." Blossom was an unapologetic classist. I said hello to the handsome, giddy Gopa, who smiled back. Then I turned and asked Blossom if her friend from Israel was at the party. "She will be here later, and yes, I want you to hear her story." Blossom continued talking with Gopa, "The early Buddhists considered death as part of the continuum of life."

Looking down, I saw that all of Blossom's bedding was in deep maroon tones. I laughed to myself, gently touching the comforter, as I remembered her screeching to all of us, "Penis and vagina, penis and vagina. This is why everything must be crimson red!" I later learned that one of her doctors had told her she would probably die of a heart attack or a massive hemorrhage. Her real motivation was for her blood to match the color of the sheets, should it be the latter.

I was sitting at Blossom's feet, near her oxygen tank. Suri had quietly entered the room and sat on the other side of the bed near Gopa. I felt a slight tension between them. Suddenly Blossom's friend Zipporah, from Israel, arrived. After some introductions, Blossom started cackling and waving her arms toward the end of the bed, "The four exotics, the four exotics!" She wanted the four of us to stand at the foot of her bed in a row. Compliantly, Gopa, Suri, Zipporah, and I lined up behind the sleigh bed's curved lower footrest. Her inner bright light was reflecting on us, reminding us that we are love. We stood there smiling, arms around shoulders, knowing this was a special moment for Blossom. I had never felt like an *exotic*; I was not from another country like the others, I was an American Jew. Is this what she meant by including me in this group? Whatever her thinking, I was honored and happy to be standing with her treasured friends at such a poignant time in her life, most likely her last Christmas. Someone quickly snapped a picture of us.

Blossom grew tired and asked for some quiet. I wandered back to the living room. The tiny house was stuffed like a sardine can. I spotted a bald man sitting in the dining area on a small wooden circular chair, his face in his hands. Was this her beloved Colonel? Paul, her high school sweetheart? The soldier with many stars and awards for military combat? There was no question that he was shaken.

I pulled up a chair next to him, sat down, introduced myself, and asked him what was so troubling. He asked, "Is it possible to love two women at the same time?" He continued, "I have probably lost my family tonight. By choosing to be in Austin, instead of in Virginia with them, I am going to be rejected, if not worse."

"Are you married?" I asked.

His reply sounded perfunctory, "Yes, for almost fifty years! When my daughter and wife found out that I was taking care of Blossom, I was thrown out of the house." Before me, I saw a man quite successful in his career, as he had achieved the status of full colonel, who also had competing priorities in his personal life. He seemed quite down and full of despair. He partially shielded his sky-blue eyes as he spoke to me. I wondered in my realization, *Where is this "top man" whom Blossom always raves about?*—and if he was often this open with a stranger. Our conversation was cut short by events.

Gopa pranced into the small living room and said that it was time for a group Hu. He wanted everyone to hold hands, shut their eyes, and meditate on the word *Hu*. The Hu meditative chant is short for *Huwa*, a name for God in Sufism. Literally it is the third-person pronoun for Allah in both Hebrew and Arabic. I grasped Paul's hand on one side and the hand of another member of the group on the other as we began a long, five-minute holy chant to the Lord Almighty, alive all around us, in a dying woman's house. The circle of people snaked around the front rooms, down the hallway, into the main bedroom, back to the apartment, and up again to the living room. Paul joined in with everyone. The air resounded with our searing but hopeful noise. It was an exhilarating five minutes. I later went to tell Blossom she was wrong about what she had once told me regarding her Colonel—he did know how to meditate.

The evening ended soon after. People started going into Blossom's chamber to thank her and kiss her goodbye. Suri was in the living room, arguing with Paul about American politics and her horror of a presidential infidelity. I didn't engage; I was ready to leave. This had been a bit too much social face for me, and I longed for more intimate communications with trusted dear ones and family. I convinced Suri that it was time to go. I drove back to my parking area, and Suri got into her car. I climbed the steps to the second floor, retreating to my apartment and the well of my studious life. It had been a Christmas celebration like no other I had ever experienced. This unusual event, hosted by a woman at the end of her life who generously engaged with praise and hospitality, had been a gift for all who attended. I felt great happiness for Blossom that so many people cared about her and chose to spend their Christmas afternoon and evening with her.

CHAPTER 8

MAKING THE DEATH CHART

After the winter holidays, Blossom asked me to use my astrological skills to discover when she might die. I had never received such a request and thought it was beyond my training. But I told her I would fool around with my astrology computer program and see what I could discover.

I could not see anything obvious when I checked the usual reference points in Blossom's natal chart. However, as luck would have it, I was casually listening to an old astrology tape, and one of the instructors suggested checking on Jupiter's current movement against the natal chart. To that observer, Jupiter's transit was another possible indicator of the end of life due to its massive amount of fire. I went back to my original work and saw that on April 12, 1999, transiting Jupiter was going to be ninety degrees from, or at the midpoint of, the always opposing South and North nodes in Blossom's chart. I thought: *It's time for Blossom to pay the piper, karmic debt at one node and the great beyond at the other! And Jupiter lights the match!* Then I had a flash: it was not luck that I had re-listened to that particular tape, but a perfect example of Jung's concept of synchronicity! His idea was that events are not always connected by causation but by meaning. What made me choose that tape on an unrelated topic and why on this day was I searching for the year's astrological events? The two events were meant to be important and informative to each other, to connect their meanings.

When I went to present my results to Blossom, she had her beads on the bed and quickly picked them up to put them on. She realized that I did not know the significance of these beads, so she explained what they were. *Japamala* or *mala*, Sanskrit for "garland," is a string of prayer beads. Similar to using rosary beads, wearing Mala beads is ornamenting oneself in spirituality. Brown or red mala beads, also used in Hinduism, Buddhism, and other Eastern religions, can be part of one's meditation practice. Blossom was rarely seen without her deep-red necklace. I thanked her for explaining her ritual to me. She became quite giddy yet also circumspect.

"What did you find? When will I die?"

I responded that we needed to move to the front dining area so that we could use the table. She complied. I opened my folder and placed two charts on the table: her natal chart and a second chart of the planets' positions on April 12, 1999, placed around her natal chart. I would usually begin by explaining a few qualities of the natal chart, but Blossom was taken with the beauty of its geometric design.

"I want to hang this up! It is so beautiful. I love it!"

Blossom was a Virgo, born September 11, 1926. I oriented her to the chart and showed her how there were two planets in her fifth house, which corresponded to her two children. She did not really want a review of her qualities or her personality as reflected in the chart. She knew who she was and what she had lived. Therefore, I suggested we move on to the chart with the two wheels, one inside the other. I pointed out that the inner wheel was her natal chart, the same design as we had first looked at. The wheel around it showed the position of the planets in the solar system on April 12, 1999.

"Why that date?"

"Do you see this symbol? It looks almost like a number four. That symbol represents Jupiter and its placement at the time you were born. Jupiter, the king of the gods, the largest planet in our solar system, is a fireball. Now, look at the outer wheel. Can you see this U-shaped figure and, directly across from it, an upside-down U? Both of them are at thirteen degrees, as is Jupiter. They are communicating with each other! I am thinking this may be the day by which you will have made your transition."

Blossom asked me tentatively, "So, I will die in spring? This is what my hospice advisor told me, contrary to the three months the doctors gave me last September." She became elated! She started singing, "I will die in spring; I die in spring. And what a lovely time of year to die, just before Easter this year."

I was feeling unsettled and ready to put the whole thing to the side. I tried to remind her that we had to be cautious, as her body had a mind of its own! But Blossom trusted the information explicitly and considered me to be the oracle at that moment. She thanked me profusely.

So many events happened in the next few months that soon Blossom and I completely forgot about this prognostication. I continued my calls and visits to Blossom's. One day in February, I saw a new health supplement on her nightstand. It was Hawaiian Noni liquid. No sooner had I entered the hallway when Blossom excitedly announced that Henry had appeared and was staying at the house.

"Is he here?" I asked.

"No, he has taken the car and is out shopping."

I could not wait to meet this young man, now in his mid-thirties.

THE DRAMATIC SESTET

CHAPTER 9

THE MEDITATION GROUP

Henry was a whirlwind, no question. He arrived shortly with a few bags in his arms and walked right by, barely acknowledging his mother or me. Blossom asked him what the matter was.

"I had trouble parking. It was so congested; there were no parking spaces."

He stormed around, unpacking and banging his items on the stove and surfaces in the kitchen. Blossom waited until he was settled and then introduced him to me. I said, "Hello."

He finally looked at me, and I caught a glimpse through his black-rimmed glasses of a troubled, almost scowling face. But he straightened to the demands of the moment and began to relax. He turned and asked his mother, "Are you taking your Noni juice?"

"Of course! Every day," Blossom replied.

Henry turned back toward the small kitchen, and Blossom and I returned to sit in the living room. Henry decided to make himself a sandwich and avoid talking with us.

Blossom paid no mind. She was excited to tell me about a meditation group she was attending and anxious to invite me to its next meeting. *Invite* is putting it mildly. I had become one of Blossom's running buddies, and she fully expected me to make the time for her priorities! Reluctant as usual to disrupt my routine, I urged myself to experience more of her activities, as her world fit my life interests. The following Tuesday we went together, and it turned out to be the right decision. I was fascinated with the people, their energy, and their group leader, Jacob. He began that evening by reminding the group of the usual format: seven to nine, every other Tuesday night. Then he gave an outline of the evening's schedule.

That night, for a prompt, he told some childhood stories about his introduction to esoteric Christianity. This was to help us paint a mental picture before we became silent and began to meditate. We sat quietly in a large circle for a very long time. Jacob had asked a member of the group to lead us in a guided meditation. In a few moments' time, a woman began to speak. She had us imagine one of our favorite places. She continued, slowly and deliberately:

> Begin walking from your special place on the worn path up a gradual hill. You are entering a more wooded area as you climb. Up ahead, there in the middle of the path, is a tree stump glowing with light. There is a small box on the stump as you approach it, and you see that it has your name on it. Pick up the box and open it. In it, you will find the one gift you have been hoping and praying for! Put the gift back in the box and carry it with you back down to your favorite place. Take it home with you. Cherish this gift.

We returned to complete silence. Jim brought us out of our deep thoughts about a half hour later. He asked us to share any visions we had experienced. I assumed Blossom would jump at the opportunity to share and educate, based on her knowledge and experience in the Eastern traditions. But she remained strangely silent.

I took Blossom home and walked her up the crooked stairway. She wanted to show me a poem before I went back to my apartment. The poem was "In Praise of a Living Guru," about her Professor. It was a short, twelve-line poem, which praised his unique abilities:

> You walked with me for twenty-five years.
> You gave me all the goodness and kindness in your soul.
> You were the "open handed one",
> Now you no longer walk next to me.
> Yet, you are here, around me.
> Your bright moon face stays before me.
> I hear your voice in my ear.
> I have been carried on your shoulders beneath the seas,

To learn your water world.
Dream away in your time of reflection and wonder.
Thank you for your magic gifts.
Thank you for your blessings.
(B. Burns 1991)

I had seen this poem on Kyle's altar, but I indulged Blossom and let her read it to me to hear her emphases. I didn't try to connect this poem with what we experienced at Jacob's group meditation, but I had failed to realize Blossom may have gone into deep thought about missing her Professor. They had built the prayer room together; they had meditated together. Blossom finished reading her tribute. She seemed to be saying: *This is the real thing. He understands. And I understand him.*

This evening was different from my other visits and outings with Blossom. She was not eager to teach and share with the world. I had assumed because she had years of daily meditation practice spent in her prayer room that she would find some way to educate others. I had also assumed that she would be thinking about her deceased son. She had raved and insisted that this was *the* meditation group to go to, yet upon reflection, I did not find it different from any other meditation experience I had up to that point. Many of the yoga classes I took had several moments of meditation to begin and end, and I had heard versions of the speaker's metaphoric story in the past, but I did not experience any breakthrough when silent. What was different was attending such an event with Blossom and seeing her in a new light. She could be quiet, she could be internally busy, she could be a participant. So, I was exposed to another part of her. I felt our friendship deepened not from the act of going but from the result of going. Afterward, she shared the love and joy of being the chosen mentee to her Professor and read her poem of gratitude for her mentor to me. This was her gift, a few moments of sharing her internal experience. Oh, to have seen this adoration in real time, to have experienced Blossom and the Professor's unique relationship. I would have liked to make my own appraisal of the Professor, to see in my own way what was unusual about him. But it could not happen. Nevertheless, she was stamping it into my brain: find a worthy person, study with them, learn from their wisdom, and finally, go out and teach the world.

I went to this meditation group two more times on my own, as Blossom did not feel well enough to go again with me. And the last time I attended was with the Colonel, at the beginning of May.

CHAPTER 10

A Midweek Evening, A Weekend Afternoon

I had established a rhythm of two visits with Blossom per week. This seemed to fit well with my course preps and commute back and forth to San Marcos. I drove to Blossom's on a midwinter Tuesday evening. She had stopped going to the meditation group because she had begun chemotherapy treatments, which made her too exhausted to go out. I was listening to the car radio that had a program on goddesses. I listened briefly and loved it, so I bounded into Blossom's studio and said, "Let's turn to NPR on the radio because they are having a program on the goddesses." Blossom had some 1940s music on. She indulged me and tuned her radio to the correct channel. I was enjoying the review, smiling and nodding my head looking directly at Blossom, while she stared back, enjoying it, too. And then she abruptly exclaimed, "We already know all of this! I'm turning it off." So that was that. Stunned, I wondered what was next on her agenda.

There was no escaping her worsening condition. She was on and off her large oxygen tank, and she was thrilled when someone had been able to get her a smaller, travel-size tank on wheels. She had me drive her to the doctor, and her oncologist, and when we returned home, I rubbed salve on her sores. This was quite a different role for me from the turn of the year. This was more intimate. Blossom was not calling me much anymore, because she was so exhausted in the evenings. I had to reach out or stop by. Her decline in late February seemed so rapid.

One Saturday morning we watched *The Tomb of the Unknown*. Geralyn, the Jungian Diplomate analyst, was already there, embellishing the narrative with her recent trip to Egypt. Blossom asked about mummification—removing the moisture—as it was discussed on the show. They spoke about Giza, the death of the sun god Ra, the tourists' climb through the queen's pyramid burial chamber "like snakes," Blossom interjected, and the tomb of Osiris. Motivated by her love of Egyptian culture and spirituality, Geralyn shared that she and a few other Jung members had formed the Isis Institute. She spoke about how it had created a new energy and was taking on a life of its own, stating with unmistakable finality that the Isis Institute was for women only. Blossom and Geralyn agreed that men did not like intellectual women. And the two of them did not care one iota!

"My ex-husband was a perfect example of this," Blossom said.

After Geralyn left, Blossom shared with me that her dentist husband had raped her when they were dating. I was nonplussed. She began, "During this era, women were forced or shamed into marrying their rapists! I saw no other way, and I married Kingston. I had two sons with him, and this helped me have a purpose in the marriage. But Kingston and I lived in two different worlds, and he did not value my opinions or my well-being." She continued, my eyes and ears wide open. "Can you imagine? An artist and a dentist? We even ate completely different foods. And he had nothing to do with the children!"

"Blossom, we each must survive our childhoods and try to choose a marriage partner we can respect and hopefully love. Did you find anything attractive about him? You must have, originally!"

"I thought he was an intellectual! What a mistake."

Blossom was tired and did not want to talk anymore. The visit from Geralyn, watching the show, the private talk of her past with me—all this drained her. She lay down in her bed.

"Okay, beautiful, I see you need your rest after such an active morning. I will round up my things and continue my day. I will call to check on you later today," I explained.

She gave me a small nod of her head. By the time I reached the outer steps, I was already deep in my dismay about her statements on rape. I had heard about this phenomenon of women marrying their rapists, but I could not believe that my brilliant Blossom would have fallen into that cultural trap! I was shaking my head and wearing a pained face, struggling to understand this story, as I got into my car.

Driving away, I quickly realized Blossom was at present comfortable, and she had shared something new: her attraction to the culture of death rituals of the Egyptian royals. She knew it was important to honor deaths as important events unto themselves. Blossom had no fear—for one, because she trusted her circle of caregivers to honor her death.

CHAPTER 11

The Sleigh Bed Soiree

It was the end of February on a mild Austin winter day. I drove to visit Blossom and felt hopeful. Blossom's chemotherapy treatments were finished. She was beginning to shape up again.

I walked in and sat down at the side of her bed. She explained with delight that the Colonel was here! I asked where. She said he was out shopping. We chatted about how she was feeling and who had been visiting and staying over. I tried to broach a local political issue, but Blossom had no opinion nor interest in it. Instead, she pivoted and began to talk about the therapy treatments and her childhood.

"I was unloved by my mother and father as a child and adolescent."

"Why?"

"I was a surly child, moody and intense. I preferred writing poetry to participating in sports. School was too easy for me. I was bored, and I did well without studying. I know this kind of childhood turned me into an artist. I put all my thoughts and feelings into my work."

"Were you painting and drawing at that time?"

"No, I was writing poetry and prose. I once wrote a book report on a made-up story for a class. It was called "Pure Innocent Love, A Mystery." The teacher pulled me aside after reading it. He said it was publication caliber. I knew I was an advanced thinker."

Suddenly we heard the outer door of the mudroom push open and then the inner door to the hallway. Blossom looked at me and smiled, her apple cheeks almost popping off her face, "That's the Colonel!" He never advanced to the bedroom, just peeked around the wall and waved at Blossom. I did not get a view of him, as I was seated facing Blossom. He said he was going into the kitchen and would be back in a minute. We continued our discussions about childhood trauma and its effects. Blossom shared one more troubling event. Her one sibling, a brother, had died in his adulthood, further isolating her in the family.

She asked me, "What made you become a scholar?" There were many factors contributing to the answer. But I chose to tell her, "My grandfather told me at four years old that I might be lucky enough one day to have a PhD. And I asked him, 'What's that?' I had trouble understanding his explanation. But in every school course I took, and every job I had, I was always being encouraged by the professionals to continue my studies. By later adulthood, one has an idea one wishes to explore further. Eventually, it seemed the only path forward."

The Colonel approached the room slowly because he was carrying a tray. He moved to the right side of Blossom's bed where there was an armchair. He had a cutting board with apple and pear slices, and cheeses, displayed in a wheel. I noticed his design and complimented him. A playfulness seemed to enter the room with him. He enjoyed playing "the waiter" to his beloved Blossom and to me, the corners of his mouth curling as he attempted to suppress a smile, placing the treats gracefully in the middle of the bed. The Colonel and I were happy we were both there, so we could get to know each other a bit more. We had each heard about the other from Blossom and had a short conversation at her Christmas party.

Blossom began to cackle about how she could see my past and future. We had spoken earlier about my childhood, so I didn't question her knowledge of my past. But I had no idea what she was intimating about my future.

Paul and Blossom decided it was time to start singing songs. Blossom began singing "We Wish You a Merry Christmas" and followed it with other holiday songs. She was displaying one of her main dictums: Every day is Christmas. Although it was midwinter, this was how she treated gifts and birthdays. Any day is fine for a present and your birthday! It was Paul's turn next and he led us in "Auld Lang Syne." It seemed to be a small gift from his heart to hers. When it was my turn, I chose a song we had all learned as kids, "If I Had a Hammer." Then Blossom rushed into "Silent Night." Around and around we went, finishing the treats as we giggled and sang. I felt such love in this merriment.

I realized it was late and said I had to leave. That seemed to be Blossom's cue, and she blurted out: "I am willing Paul to Regina!"

What? I looked at her with a quizzical face. Paul completely ignored her and politely offered to help me to my car. She repeated this declaration again. I thought she was acting completely crazy or was confused, and I chose not to talk with her about this. Instead, I said goodbye to Blossom while Paul returned the empty tray to the kitchen. It had become entirely dark outside, so he took the flashlight. Before I got into my car I asked,

"How long will you be here this visit?"

"Until the end of the week."

I thought, *Good. I can fit in a visit once more before he leaves.* It was like being touched by a magic wand to be included in this spontaneous play between Blossom and Paul. I cherished these moments of intimacy with my new friends, flashing a huge smile as I said goodbye.

CHAPTER 12

THE NEIGHBORHOOD TEA

Once again, my work was interrupted by a phone call from Blossom. It was the beginning of March, and I was preparing midterm exams for my students. She said she was having a tea party the following Saturday afternoon at two and that she would like me to serve the tea. At this point in our relationship, I did not think to ask her what was up; I readily agreed. I reminded her I would be seeing clients in the morning and would be finished by one or two in the afternoon. I agreed to come over as soon as I was through. I did not know that the president of the Jung, Leon, had put out the call to help Blossom prepare for her weekend event. He was hoping several members would wash the windows of the upstairs house and clean up the yard before guests arrived.

When I arrived at Blossom's studio house, there was no one inside. I turned around, went out through the Japanese side garden, and continued up the stairs to the big house, a rectangular dwelling built into the bamboo forest, all of it looking out and over the studio extending down to Shoal Creek. Blossom was seated at the center of the living room with chairs arranged around her in a semicircle. Most of the neighbors were there. Dr. Ochs, a retired pediatrician who lived on the north side of Blossom, was chatting with Mr. Bailey, a clothier of menswear who lived on the south side. All three of them were looking out the floor-to-ceiling windows and could view the passersby who were enjoying the bike and walking trails along this side of the creek. Another guest was one of the two women who were raising a baby together and lived at the mouth of the small street. She was talking with the neighbor whose house was directly across the street from Blossom's, a mother who lived with her teenage son. And last, there was Stephen, an elderly man who lived in between the mother and the tailor, who grew roses in a large garden plot across the street from his home. He was sipping tea quietly.

I went into the kitchen to fix a pot of tea, and while the water was boiling, I spread shortbread cookies and lemon bars on two plates for the guests. I was fumbling around, trying to be helpful but not knowing my true role in this group of neighbors and feeling like an outsider. I took a few breaths and carried on with my duties, reentering the large living room to serve tea and cookies. The neighbors were engaged in conversation in several small groups, waiting for the main event. Shortly after, Blossom tapped a spoon on her teacup. She stood up, using her cane for support, and began to address the group. "I have invited you all here today because, as you know, I am dying." She paused to give the neighbors time to register this knowledge. "I have wanted to leave something for the good of the community, and I have decided to give my two houses and my property and assets to a foundation. This foundation will provide a place for women to meet and to hold classes and lectures free of charge. I am working out the details with my attorney." The neighbors remained stunned and began looking at each other for a response. Finally, the two men who were adjacent neighbors began expressing concern.

Dr. Ochs asked, "Is this going to be some kind of *safe house?*"

"No, not at all; that is not my intention, as safe houses already exist in Austin."

"I object right now to your home being left for abused and battered women," Mr. Bailey exclaimed in a loud and angry voice, "I have children living on this street and I do not want them near that kind of woman."

"What kind of woman is that?" Blossom began raising her voice in kind.

"Women who have been abused or raped," answered Dr. Ochs.

Blossom roared to her feet and began yelling at the group. "I have been an abused woman! I've been raped twice in my life! Do you want to see an abused woman? You are looking at one. Are you afraid of sitting in a room with me? All women from every level of society are abused women." Her creamy white skin had turned crimson by now. She was visibly fuming. She yelled, "I have no time to waste in my numbered last days!" Then she delivered her final blow to the group: "I didn't have to invite you here and ask you to give me your blessing. But I thought that would be the neighborly thing to do. I am telling you now that this is what I am going to do! And I don't care if you like it or not."

With this, she picked up her small oxygen tank and began wheeling it toward the front door, cane in her other hand. I had been standing at the living room and kitchen archway, and Blossom grabbed my upper arm for support on her way out the front door. I walked her steadily down the rickety steps of the main house and over to the shale pathway to her studio. She was still sputtering with rage. Once we entered her studio, she really let it all out.

"The nerve of these people! They have broken every covenant we originally agreed to. Ochs built a boathouse and semi-circular drive to park his boat on the park side of the street; Stephen built his garden beds, and Bailey put in a swimming pool and changing house, not to mention the swing set for the kids to play on every day after school. Did any of them ever ask me what I thought about their plans? Did any of them stop to consider how their structures were changing the environment, the neighborhood, or the quality of the view on our street? Hypocrites, all of them, hypocrites!"

I knew I was not supposed to answer any of these questions and continued to guide Blossom into her crowded bedroom. I helped her take off her black clothing, black cowboy boots, and jewelry and change into her lounge clothes. She had not expected opposition to her plans. Her response had been spontaneous. Soon she was back in bed and worried she had raised her blood pressure with all her yelling. I patted her forearm and began rubbing it to calm her down. I returned the oxygen tank to its stand in the open closet area. Her big blond bouffant seemed to wrap itself around her face and seek rest as well.

I did not see the neighbors leave the upstairs house, but I knew Leon would conduct the party's closure so that every person felt relatively stabilized. I went back upstairs to check on its condition and clean up and then returned to say goodbye to Blossom. She was already sleeping. As the afternoon came to its close, I was dismayed that the men who had monopolized the response to Blossom's plans were blaming women for experiences of sexual violence and ignored her stated intention for a safe space for women to learn. None of the women in the group had a moment to express to Blossom how generous and unusual her ideas were. I felt bad for Blossom that her good gestures had been turned upside down. Time would show me, though, that this initial opposition would only fuel her fire more intensely: the tea party had refined her commitment to the foundation.

CHAPTER 13

Soon after, Blossom experienced pains in her heart. She felt as if a knife were stabbing her and an elephant was sitting on her chest. She was taken to Christopher House, the hospice house in Austin. She called the Colonel in Virginia, and he was there in two days. She called me, and I was there in an instant. When I entered her room, Blossom recounted what had happened, explaining that the hospice's trained workers would help to interweave her healing community of fifty years with their workers to provide her compassionate care and dignity throughout her dying. In the meantime, Ned had sent an email to the caregivers, the Jungians, and a few others of Blossom's cherished friends, explaining her move to hospice and informing everyone the Colonel would be arriving tomorrow. He attached the latest update of Blossom's funeral plans, which he and Blossom had been working on since February. Blossom spent twenty-three days at Christopher House, convalesced, and returned home to the studio. From that moment on, Blossom had a lot to say.

Her episode at hospice caused her to make some big decisions. She moved forward with her plans for the foundation, a project which now consumed every waking moment. She decided to donate her houses to the Isis Institute and the Jung Society so that women could be served in a gift economy. When I asked what a *gift economy* was, she responded, "There is a woman at the university, named Geneva, who has written a paper and made a video project on the gift economy. I read about this, called her up, and invited her over to learn more about this system of payment." Blossom and Geneva quickly became close friends, and Blossom eagerly signed as a witness to Geneva's operating expense document for the foundation.

The whole of Blossom's approach to broadening the meaning of her life reminded me of my grandfather Gerstman. If he read a story in the morning newspaper about a family down on their luck, he would call them up, invite them for lunch at his apartment or his club, and give them the finances they needed to get back on their feet. This was his version of the gift economy. My grandfather was participating in a practice of giving while living; Blossom was participating in a practice of giving while dying. Gramps had a painful and fairly quick death in a hospital, isolated, while hooked up to machines. Blossom was working to avoid that scenario. Her preparation for her death was organized and methodical, as well as compassionate and connected. Blossom involved her community in her journey toward her death. She was rarely alone! The Jungians and IANDS members became her caretakers and the larger Austin community her students whom she taught a different response to illness and impending death. She showed us the critical role that the thriving can and should play in the lives of those on the decline.

The following Saturday, Blossom set out to fully explain to me the events in her life of the past few weeks, including letting me know that the Colonel was still in town since her hospice stay. She explained the ideal situation for her foundation: "No one pays for the classes and services at my foundation; they repay with a gift of their own. For example, if you take a yoga class, you donate an hour of therapy services." The Colonel made us lunch, which for Blossom was the same every day: six crackers with pimento cheese on them and some tea. She leaned toward me, "Eats like a dog," glancing at Paul. I suppressed a laugh. I understood this comment in light of his military career. Apparently, he had experienced four days with no food when fighting in the Korean War.

Blossom continued, "Hannah had come over to visit shortly after the meeting with the neighbors. I explained my idea of how the foundation would operate. Hannah told me immediately, 'You can't do it because of the financial problems!'" Blossom was stunned to be facing opposition from one of her trusted advisors. They argued and Blossom, in her dramatic authoritarian way, offered to take out her checkbook and write Hannah a check right then and there if that would bring her on board! Blossom relived the moment.

"Hannah was a *brick*. She left without our usual warmth and affection. I felt disillusioned and betrayed. The next day I collapsed, ending up in an ambulance and at Christopher House. It hurt my feelings so much. While there, Geneva visited me, and I knew the *giving way* was the way to go. I told her, thinking of JFK, 'Ask not what your country can do for you, but what you can do…!' When I think of some women, battered physically, emotionally, and spiritually, they need to get a sense of identity. They need a group of awakened, forward women. As Geneva says, when you give unilaterally, you are other-oriented. Gift-giving creates bonds. It satisfies needs and creates a *community*. It's Latin: *co* (together), *muni* (of service), *ty* (unity). Women's hormones are different because they have the babies; they must give and the baby cannot give back. It's not the woman's biology that is the cue, it's the baby's! Whereas a man is not taught that from childhood. As a result, a man's identity fits in with the exchange market versus a woman's identity, which is other-oriented. After I returned from hospice, Hannah returned to the studio with two other board members from the Jung: Geralyn and Yani. They wanted me to call the lawyer and rewrite the papers. In sum, they were not willing to work for free! They were so used to making the big bucks as analysts, they refused to do sessions for those who could not pay. What hypocrisy! These were three of my soldiers, and they betrayed the plan."

On hearing the story, I could feel Blossom's sense of betrayal and disappointment. Every move she made, she received preliminary approval from these two friends. And now, at a pivotal moment, they had abandoned her. Adding to the rejection by the neighbors, she was wounded. Yet she had a rare ability to transform the moment. The Colonel came in, and Blossom angrily blurted out to us, "I have $120,000 in the bank to carry it all out.

And I have a Hindu temple in Bombay that I inherited from G. V. Desani." That was the first I'd heard about that!

Paul suggested, "Then ask for donated funds, for your operating costs."

After lunch, Geneva visited Blossom to write her will. Blossom began to dictate: "I donate $1,100 per month to the Blossom Foundation." Blossom elucidated that this money was for the normal expenses and upkeep of the house and its grounds. She stated the general rules of the gift economy and her inner philosopher concluded the text: "All Buddhist texts end, 'for the good of the many.' End the will with that phrase."

The Colonel and I witnessed the paper. Lastly, she had Geneva write: "It is with love and in the spirit of the great goddess that this gift is given and is accepted by the Blossom Foundation. The gift of giving grows with each loving gift and humankind, and womankind is enriched."

The will was short, it accomplished her goals, and Blossom, I noticed, made no mention of her one living son or the Colonel. Geneva and I got ready to leave. She told Blossom, "I will get these notes and signatures typed up and deliver them to your attorney."

Blossom was so grateful. A pronounced peace came over her face and she relaxed back in her bed. The Colonel remained by her side. I was not only a document's signature witness but also a witness to an elder on a mission as she made her culminating dream a reality.

CHAPTER 14

THE FINAL SESSIONS

The next time I visited Blossom, she had just taken her morphine. She mentioned the chemo burn was resolving and that there had been a lot of company arriving each day since she had returned home. She told me she had a catheter in her heart because of a *little* infection she had suffered when in hospice. She surprised me when she said seemingly out of the blue, "I wonder what happened to the boy who was in the fatal car crash with my son. I keep my Tibetan prayer flag up by Kyle's altar. Go up to the front office and find my *Tibetan Book of the Dead*. I want you to read it to me." I retrieved the book and started reading out loud. Blossom interrupted me shortly, "It's Tuesday night and you need to go to Jacob's meditation group! I long to go, but I can't manage it. But you should go. It is the wisdom of the ages. He's just passing it along. Please go."

I knew a caregiver was expected soon. I sighed with exasperation and, resigned, turned to pick up my purse. "OK. Goodbye, Blossom. See you this weekend."

I visited Blossom during the first week of April. A nurse was there treating spots on Blossom's cheek and nose. She changed the bandages and refilled Blossom's prescriptions. We listened to a tape on Egyptian mysteries. Blossom asked, "How is your teaching going? And what has happened to Suri? I think she has big control issues!" She then swiftly turned to the coming holidays, "What about Easter and Passover? What are your plans? I have no family of significance. I am not into eating. All holidays are BS to me because each day is Christmas!"

"I know Blossom! You tell me that all the time." Blossom had earlier confronted me, and Suri at another time, about not including the other in an activity. When I explained I was spending time with another friend, she fought with me suggesting I was negligent or mean but then quieted down. So, what happened to Suri was Blossom and her nosy ideas! She had tried to tell each of us what to do, and that simply would not fly. *So, Ms. Burns, who is the woman with control issues?*

I returned to Blossom's to attend an organizational meeting of the main players in the nascent foundation. It was the Colonel's last night. Geralyn was there. Blossom was using her oxygen. Karl had called, another of Blossom's dearest friends. He was discussing a personal problem with Blossom. At one moment Blossom turned and stated proudly to me, "So, you have a little Artemis in you after all!" I did not understand her reference to me or my behavior. Perhaps my stance on Suri in our earlier conversation lingered in her mind. I had pushed against her ideas, like the decisive goddess, and would not budge. A first.

Blossom continued to talk. "I gave the artist Ben Nichols my paint brushes when he took me to the downtown Omni to view his yellow mural."

I was startled. "You went out to the Omni with Ben since you've been home?"

"And Leon is bringing boxes with the Jung Society's library into the upstairs house this Saturday."

"I'd like to tell you about a couples' group I visited, Blossom."

"Later, as I am thinking right now of Aphrodite, with her little baby, who is now Demeter. And her husband only wants Aphrodite! Her thinking was like mine when I realized I had to leave Kingston, 'You are not the same person I married!'"

"No kidding, Blossom."

"Yeah, LIFE!"

This disjointed conversation, the increased interruptions, and the attempts to control the flow were now the norm between us. I felt a sense of loss, but I understood the changes the brain makes as it prepares to die. I was an observer. I was a nonjudgmental friend. Blossom still possessed her incredible intellect and I felt honored to be welcomed by her and engage with her.

Before I left, Blossom asked me if I would be interested in the resident caretaker job for the Blossom Foundation: "I want someone to live here in the studio and monitor the foundation activities upstairs. It would be rent-free in exchange for handling the mail, coordinating with Isis, making their schedule known to the public, and jobs like that. Most especially I want to be certain that no exchange of money occurs for services provided."

This request came as a total surprise to me. I did not consider myself a worker bee for Blossom and her foundation. She had the Colonel and the Jung and Isis board members for these jobs. She had not put me on the board of her new foundation. I felt a bit bewildered and responded, "I will think about this, Blossom."

As I pondered her request, I began to realize Blossom wanted to entrust me with her many personal items and to live in her sacred space. It would mark a significant turn in our friendship odyssey, which began with a magnetic attraction in a Greek restaurant that had shifted into caring for her namesake foundation, to carry out the details of her will. I was brought to a crossroads: was I willing to change my focus and add this responsibility to my life?

"Regina, I am so tired. Please refresh my water and I will drink, then take a nap."

I brought Blossom a fresh glass of water and she mumbled, "I'm looking forward to two things: ice cream Friday night with Dina and our date next Saturday."

"Yes. See you Saturday, and keep up your spirits!"

"Goodbye."

"Love you, Blossom."

THE LYRICAL COUPLET

CHAPTER 15

A SATURDAY OF SURPRISES

I called Blossom to confirm our Saturday afternoon date. Ned answered the phone.

"How auspicious."

"*What* is auspicious, Ned? What are you talking about?"

"Blossom is not breathing."

"What?! Did Blossom die?" I was jarred. I wondered if I had already experienced my last moments with her and felt a small panic.

"We aren't sure."

I felt disbelief, wanting to scream and cry at the same time. I thought, *Is this the moment we have all prepared for?* Caitlyn answered from behind him, "We really don't know."

"I'll be right over."

I rushed to get out the door. I needed to find out if Blossom was or was not breathing. I had never been the discoverer of a dead person, so I had no experience with the confusion, doubt, and disbelief involved. Arriving, I hurriedly entered, and Caitlyn and Ned called to me from the bedroom. I walked in and saw Blossom's tiny body curled in her bed, sheets pulled up to her chest, arms tucked toward her stomach. They asked me, "What do you think?" I leaned over to Blossom's nose and mouth to see if any air was passing in and out. Nothing. Then I felt her forehead. It was not yet cold, but it was not warm either. I took one of her wrists and waited for a pulse. None. This cursory exam seemed to confirm my fears. I straightened up and asked Ned to call the hospice doctor right away in order to declare her dead.

"You think she's dead?" He seemed to be in a dream state.

"Yes, Ned, Blossom is dead. How long have you been with her this morning?"

"About an hour. We thought we would check on her as we were in this part of town. The schedule says Dina was with her last night."

"Yes, Blossom was so looking forward to her ice cream date with Dina when I saw her last Tuesday. Please call Dina to see how she left Blossom this morning." I was feeling struck by lightning but seemed to know how to orchestrate these moments.

Ned called the hospice house and Caitlyn called Dina. The doctor was on his way. Dina told Caitlyn that she did not wake Blossom this morning as they had enjoyed a very late evening watching movies and eating ice cream in bed. She was quite shocked that at some time between last night and ten this morning, Blossom had died. I asked if anyone had called the Colonel. No. So, I left a message for him to call me.

"We need to call Ben, too," Ned said. He picked up his phone and Ben answered, saying he would be over in the early afternoon.

Soon afterward, the doctor arrived and we made room for him. He lifted Blossom's torso and her head fell forward. He felt her throat and then looked at his watch. "Time of death, 11:38," he recorded the time on his papers. Then he gently moved her back to a prone position on her sleigh bed. He called the hospice to send an ambulance. Ned suggested we pray together. Someone took a photo of us praying around Blossom before the ambulance came. Caitlyn, Ned, Ben, and I held hands around and across the bed. We each took a turn creating a loving message to help Blossom's soul find its path.

An hour later, two men came and removed her body. I missed her physical presence immediately. It became strangely silent and I felt robbed. *They have taken my sweet friend away!* The almost eight-month vigil was over.

Ned wanted to schedule a phone call to organize the memorial service, saying, "I am going to check a few things, like the water temperature for the studio, and make sure the upstairs house is locked up. Regina, you take Blossom's keys, as we have a set." This felt like a passing of the torch, reminding me of my nascent responsibilities.

"When I can, I will begin to clean up and handle all of this," I sighed. It seemed like a great task, but one that I had signed up for. "And Ned, someone needs to try to contact Henry."

"I will contact Blossom's attorney, and ask him to call Henry."

Trusting the attorney would make the call to Henry took a huge load off my heart. I began to breathe. I felt I had helped my two dearest friends manage the sudden shock of our loss, as Ned deftly took the lead and supervised preparations. I went home for a while to begin absorbing the day. Although these events were anticipated, I still needed time to work on assimilating them. My precious eccentric friend was gone and I felt a hollow hole in my gut.

Four of us women decided to meet at the studio at twilight: Dina, Caitlyn, Carol, and me. Carol was a longtime friend of Blossom's who had moved to New Mexico. She had become an activist to save the prairie dogs. She happened—*happened?*—to be visiting Austin at the time. We were waiting for a call from Paul. When he called, we formed a circle around Blossom's bed, held hands, put the phone in the middle of the bed, and called out attributes we were sending to him: *Strength! Courage! Light! Love! Perspective!* We carried on for a little while, attempting to help him adjust to his deep loss. Although it was anticipated, Paul was quite bereft. Later that night, I heard from him again, via email: "My thanks to you all. She is the golden tears gathered together by the angels and carried to paradise. Today has been a hard day. As I recall you came up with the twelfth of April. Today is the tenth. Uncanny." I had forgotten about my prognostication! I too was slowly realizing that the timing of Blossom's passing was quite auspicious, as Ned had said that morning. I silently wondered, *Did Blossom will her death? Was she that much of a magician?*

Ben returned a call to me, wanting to get together to grieve. When we met, he talked about his friendship with Blossom: "Blossom was a fellow artist. I used to escort her to the meditation group. It was such an honor to know Blossom, an artist-poet like myself." I recognized that Ben was of the same ilk as Blossom—using his creative gifts to contribute to humankind. Ned had asked him to read one of her poems at the memorial celebration. And then this whirling top stood up and vanished!

Gopa also returned a call to me, saying he and his father had been doing *puja*. Puja is the ceremonial worship to a deity in order to receive blessings and good fortune. He spoke about Blossom: "Blossom died the way she did because she was helping souls. From previous good acts that I have committed, like deciding to study to be a medium, Blossom gave me the opportunity for her presence." I thought his was quite a philosophical approach to the loss of a friend and teacher, reflecting the spiritual sophistication of a true Buddhist. I plodded along, keeping my schedule, yet breathing inside a buffer zone of numbness. *So, this is grief.*

A few days passed, and Ned sent an email to Paul, Jacob, and me: "I was awakened this evening/morning with a vision of Blossom directing me to remind us all that these times are meant to recognize the PERVADING JOY that surrounds us. As tired and busy as I am, it tickles me that I am infused at this midnight hour with energy and joy. It was a gift to be the one who found her body curled up like a cozy baby with her *teddy bear* at her side." I too was very grateful it had been Ned who found Blossom as he had considerable experience with death and, more importantly, he had loved and valued Blossom for many years. Ned proceeded to share the details of Blossom's funeral arrangements. He had procured the Chapel of the Children for the first of May at ten in the morning for the memorial celebration. Blossom had installed several stained-glass windows there, which were melded into one large window at the rear entrance of the chapel. At this point, the community that Blossom had breathed her heart and soul into came together to manage every detail of her funeral and to take care of the perfunctory but necessary tasks of a death. The principal members of Blossom's inner circle met to work through the details for the funeral service. We were seeking, in Ned's words, a semblance of harmonious resonance, offering the wisdom that "joy is contagious and grief is a gift that leads to joy."

In my anguish, I was still trying to piece together Blossom's last hours. A hint came from Geo, another of Blossom's friends. I had heard from Ned that Blossom had told Geo: "I am finished, I have done everything I have to do." Whereas, the Monday evening before she died, she had told me that she still had things to do before dying. I imagine she was protecting me from the pain of loss. I was anxious to hear what Geo had to say. He confirmed Blossom had told him if she were to die now, that would be OK. She told him there were things she could still do, but what really had to be done was taken care of. I trusted Geo's reply and understood her last statement to him. I loved his depiction of Blossom as: "Surrounded by wonderful people, her *Grand Central Station* social scene."

There were three weeks between Blossom's death and her memorial service. Although I had tried to piece together all the moments of her final days and hours, I let it go and slowly accepted that I could not redo it or control it—I had lost a precious friend. Every time I walked Town Lake, swam at Barton Springs, or spent time reading, my mind wandered back to Blossom's unusual intelligence, its breadth, and depth. What a light she shone! I had not known anyone like her, suffusing every encounter with her timeless wisdom and insight. Her death left a hole in my life, as it did for many others. Although I was feeling so woefully unresolved, I thanked the universe for putting her across my path. *Grief and gratitude, grief and gratitude.* I could hear Blossom chanting in her prayer room.

CHAPTER 16

THE MEMORIAL CELEBRATION OF LIFE

The weather was wet and stormy on the first of May. Leaving my apartment before the service, I saw a cardinal and thought, *There's Blossom watching me.* An old Polynesian proverb flitted across my mind: "All great journeys begin with a storm." I felt a nervous energy as I drove to the chapel. From a distance, I could see the giant stained-glass windows, which extended from floor to ceiling, at the back of the chapel where one entered. At the service, I kept looking for her, or a sign from her. We all talked about feeling her presence. I sat down next to Dina. As I looked around, I saw that most of the people in attendance were Blossom's female friends and some of their partners. I was looking for the friends I had introduced to Blossom who had come into her world: Suri and Ann. Much like the first night I met Blossom at the Greek restaurant, I felt separated from my closest companions and was waiting for a connection with someone, to commiserate together.

Ned, who is a doctor of divinity, began the service. He gave an invocation, read a few opening prayers, and then offered some personal commentary about the life and times of Blossom Flowers Ford Burns. Next, the Colonel spoke about how Blossom's gifts were love and light: "She was the alpha and the omega of my life—I began my friendship with her in high school and finished her life with her in our seventies." Then Ben read some poems of Blossom's. I was surprised he did not choose a poem about spring and rebirth or the cycle of life. He chose, instead, simple poems that emphasized Blossom's sweetness and uncomplicated way of viewing the natural world.

Blossom's lawyer, a former State of Texas attorney general, emphasized how she was a *pioneer communicator*. This stood out in my mind from the other comments. He was referring to the fifty television shows on art history for the Fine Art Association of Texas which Blossom produced. Last, Geralyn talked about Blossom's legacy. She shared that Blossom had recently created the Blossom Foundation and the Blossom House. Friends and family also had a space before the closing to share memories. Only a few people spoke. One of them was a man who knew Blossom from their college days. He told a long story of their infrequent communications; it was clear he admired and respected her and felt a weighty loss.

I felt in two places at one time, attending to the comments and prayers while also floating under the steepled canopy. Members of Blossom's hands-on healing community were sprinkled around the sanctuary. I wondered if members of Blossom's larger community were there, those whom she invited through her newspaper articles and talks, who knew her only from her writing and ideas. Questions flooded my mind. What is truly possible to perceive as we guide a person's spirit from life to death? Are we all experiencing something akin to the medium who can communicate with those who have crossed over? Was Blossom also at two places at one time?

Together Ned and Paul read the closing prayers and invited all in the chapel to come to the studio for a party and celebration of Blossom's life. She had requested the closing song be "So Long, It's Been Good to Know Ya...," which we sang with a few tears in our eyes. The chaplain at Hospice Austin led a procession of cars to the Oakwood Cemetery where Blossom's urn was buried by a broken tree. She had purposely chosen this forlorn spot. I shook my head thinking, *Tragic and woeful, a loner to the end.* Then the chaplain led us in a graveside service. Many of us wept, but some friends were already beaming with happiness. I felt bare, with no bark to hold my fibers together, but slowly came around through group osmosis to feeling more settled.

It was around noon when most of us returned to the upstairs house—renamed the Blossom House—to celebrate her *gifts*, *guidance*, and *glory*, as Ned had written on the cover of the funeral program. The program also contained an invitation to the reception here. The foundation's work had already begun. In the big house above, a few of us watched from the windows facing the creek as a procession of people in black, and some draped in color, walked slowly down the easement from their parking spots. They seemed transfixed, almost trancelike. All of us were coming out of a somber mood, yet we also felt we were part of a magical occasion. We knew that Blossom was dancing around us, and we yearned to join her joy.

Ned shouted into the crowd in French as they entered the courtyard, "*Plus ça change, plus c'est la même chose!*"

Paul looked around and stated, "Blossom will be giggling from the urn. She was a goddess." Overall, however, he was not doing very well, pining for that final private time with Blossom before her death. It was not to be.

Although I had the warmth of knowing my last words to Blossom were *love you*, I felt such sadness that those apple cheeks and brilliant eyes would not be waiting for me on the other side of the doorway. She always welcomed me with respect and acceptance. For nine months she had stoked the fires of my mind and the affection in my heart, and now I would have to hear her voice in my imagination. I stepped out to check on the studio, and it appeared fresh and clean. Moving through its crooked hallways, I wondered what was up ahead for me. How would this emptiness I felt be filled?

Back outside, I twirled around in the courtyard. When I returned to the party, I looked around and saw a beautiful array of highly defined individuals. The house was packed with scholars and professionals, analysts and artists, poets and wanderers, and many broken hearts.

This celebration marked the passing of a pivotal figure in my life and forced me to step up a notch in the community. Shortly after this gathering, I began to prepare to move into the studio and assume the position of resident manager of the Blossom House. Once again, I returned to my solo journey on the path to enlightenment.

EPILOGUE

Since Blossom's death at home, a new certification program for becoming a death doula began in the United States. The *death doula*—what I had earlier labeled a *death transition worker*—becomes the support system present before and during hospice care, as its eyes and ears in the very end stages of caregiving for the terminally ill, providing social and emotional care in tandem with hospice's palliative care. The caregivers at Blossom's studio from 1998 to 1999 were the original death doulas, of the Blossom Flowers Ford Burns variety.

What is the sacred death? Is it the bold insistence on the lack of fear about one's death? Starting to sing when you think of your dying in spring? Or is it picking and choosing carefully how you want to spend your remaining time after a terminal diagnosis? Blossom's preparation for her death showed us many things, most especially that one's philosophy of death and dying is reflected not only in the mind but also in the body. She could have had a painful hemorrhagic event but did not. She trusted her personal and community connections and her inner thinking to complete her work. Last, she created an evening of joy with a special friend and then quietly slipped away.

The good death conjures a group of family and friends sitting quietly around an ill person, weeping when the loss occurs. In sacred death, Blossom knew we come into this life alone and we leave it alone.

DREAMS

B. BURNS 1996

Suffering in all forms
Wakens the dreamer.
Tell me of your dreams.
Where do they take you, to the stars?
Or to shining white sand hills covering
Winding caverns laid over with dripping ever
Drops dating man's small life in earth's
Deeps, within the bright ball.
Dreams move in all direction to lead
Us deeper into ourselves, deeper into what we have forgotten.
Forgotten selves moving in Time's maze of vines.
Creeping vines curl around our limbs.
Bound limbs and darken eyes, we wait.
Waiting, waiting for morning
And your new day embrace.

ACKNOWLEDGMENTS

This book began in 2005 with Karen Jones and Kathleen Brehony at their Writing Camp on Chincoteague Island, located at the tip of Virginia's Eastern Shore. They advised making posterboards for each chapter, with a word or detail around the center of each board of what belonged in that chapter. I kept those boards at the bottom of my file cabinet for sixteen years, waiting for the time and space. The COVID pandemic offered that space and in February and March 2021, I pulled out the boards and wrote *Sacred Dying*, another example of pandemic art.

Then it was the feedback at Jack Canfield and Steve Harrison's seminar "How to Get Your Book Published" in March and April 2021, which gave me the next push on this project. At that point, the entire book was fifty pages. Steve helped me see that there are two people of importance in this book! His team also advised changing the name of the manuscript to reflect who it is about.

I would like to thank Alexia Landis along with my late mother Evelyn Gerstman for their continual prodding, my dearest friend Annette Gerwitz for her certainty that many would benefit from this offering, and Sally-Ann DelVino, my lovely, brilliant editor emeritus.

To my beta readers: Bob and Emily Anderson, Ann Caldwell, Amy Steingart, Cheryl Mackin, and Edward Salisbury, a huge thank-you for taking the time, and for giving the feedback.

Robert Pruett, Ashley Barnhill, and the entire crew at Brandylane Publishers, Inc., thanks for helping me put a meaningful, small book out into the world.

And many ongoing thanks to my agent whisperer, Peter Ginsburg.

ABOUT THE AUTHOR

Dr. Regina Gerstman holds a doctorate in educational psychology from the University of Texas at Austin and taught Human Development for nine years. She is also a licensed clinical social worker who has focused on people in midlife and late life for thirty years, after more than twenty years of working in outpatient mental health. Although Blossom was the first person she spent time with while dying, she more directly participated in the caretaking of first her husband and then her mother over the next ten years when they became ill and passed away. Blossom considered Dr. Gerstman to be a scholar and included her in her inner circle ten months before her death.

www.ingramcontent.com/pod-product-compliance
Lightning Source LLC
LaVergne TN
LVHW011411080426
835511LV00005B/479